"As a vegan, the only chickens I consume are Savage's. I never miss a meal."

—Dan Piraro, *Bizarro* cartoonist

"[*Savage Chickens*] comes closer to being the heir to Gary Larson's *Far Side* than all the *Far Side* imitators in the Funny Pages of the local paper. It also channels the early *Dilbert*."

—*The Webcomic Overlook* (5 stars)

"*Savage Chickens* not only taps the heartbeat of humanity through the daily musings of workaday chickens, it also finally exposes the secret depth of office supplies! Hope in a sticky note. Pass it on."

—Summer Pierre, author of *The Artist in the Office* and *Great Gals*

D1568101

# SAVAGE CHICKENS

## A SURVIVAL KIT FOR LIFE IN THE COOP

## DOUG SAVAGE

A PERIGEE BOOK

**A PERIGEE BOOK**
**Published by the Penguin Group**
**Penguin Group (USA) Inc.**
**375 Hudson Street, New York, New York 10014, USA**
Penguin Group (Canada), 90 Eglinton Avenue East, Suite 700, Toronto, Ontario M4P 2Y3, Canada (a division of Pearson Penguin Canada Inc.) • Penguin Books Ltd., 80 Strand, London WC2R 0RL, England • Penguin Group Ireland, 25 St. Stephen's Green, Dublin 2, Ireland (a division of Penguin Books Ltd.) • Penguin Group (Australia), 250 Camberwell Road, Camberwell, Victoria 3124, Australia (a division of Pearson Australia Group Pty. Ltd.) • Penguin Books India Pvt. Ltd., 11 Community Centre, Panchsheel Park, New Delhi—110 017, India • Penguin Group (NZ), 67 Apollo Drive, Rosedale, North Shore 0632, New Zealand (a division of Pearson New Zealand Ltd.) • Penguin Books (South Africa) (Pty.) Ltd., 24 Sturdee Avenue, Rosebank, Johannesburg 2196, South Africa
Penguin Books Ltd., Registered Offices: 80 Strand, London WC2R 0RL, England

While the author has made every effort to provide accurate telephone numbers and Internet addresses at the time of publication, neither the publisher nor the author assumes any responsibility for errors or for changes that occur after publication. Further, the publisher does not have any control over and does not assume any responsibility for author or third-party websites or their content.

SAVAGE CHICKENS

First edition: March 2011

Perigee trade paperback ISBN: 978-0-399-53646-5

PRINTED IN THE UNITED STATES OF AMERICA

10   9   8   7   6   5   4   3   2   1

Most Perigee books are available at special quantity discounts for bulk purchases for sales promotions, premiums, fund-raising, or educational use. Special books, or book excerpts, can also be created to fit specific needs. For details, write: Special Markets, Penguin Group (USA) Inc., 375 Hudson Street, New York, New York 10014.

*For Janet*

## INTRODUCTION

When I was a little kid, I didn't want to be a firefighter or a doctor or an astronaut like all the other kids. I wanted to be a cartoonist.

Many years passed and, like so many others, I found myself working in an office. I wasn't quite sure how I got there, but there I was. The humming computers and overhead fluorescents made my brain twitch. My eyes hurt. My carpal tunnel hurt. The more I used a keyboard, the worse my penmanship became. Little by little, and without even noticing, I stopped drawing cartoons. Like so many childhood dreams, my cartoonist dream had faded away, replaced by the drudgery of office work. I started getting migraines: my brain's way of saying, "Hey, buddy, I didn't sign up for this."

Then, after one bad workday too many, I scribbled two chickens onto a yellow sticky note. And from then on, life improved dramatically. I had stumbled upon the secret to survival in the office world: be creative. Even if it's only for two minutes of the day. Draw, paint, sing, dance—whatever you want. Just do something creative, and you might be able to keep your brain from atrophying. You might even rediscover a childhood dream.

For me, this book is a milestone on the creative journey that saved me from a life sentence of migraine-addled office monotony. For you, I hope this book provides some laughs, a little tongue-in-cheek advice about how to survive the working world, and a few ideas to get you thinking creatively.

I hope you enjoy reading it as much as I've enjoyed drawing it!

Best,
Doug Savage

# The Morning Slog

THE MOURNING COFFEE

I CALL IT THE PROD3000. IT'S A ROBOT THAT ENHANCES PRODUCTIVITY BY 400%
WHY DOES IT HAVE A STICK WITH A NAIL THROUGH IT?
GET BACK TO WORK!
OKAY! OKAY!
DOUG SAVAGE

WELCOME TO HELL!
WHA-?? OH IT WAS JUST A DREAM - I'M AT WORK...
AAUGH!!!
DOUG SAVAGE

# How to Look Busy

lesson 2:
the fake meeting

FIRST, YOU WILL NEED ACCOMPLICES WHO ALSO WANT TO LOOK BUSY.

NEXT, FIND A MEETING ROOM WITH A GLASS WALL OR WINDOW, SO PEOPLE CAN SEE YOUR "MEETING".

OKAY, NOW TALK ABOUT WHATEVER YOU WANT.

BUT MAKE SURE YOU DON'T LAUGH TOO MUCH — YOU CAN'T LOOK LIKE YOU ARE HAVING FUN.

AND STAND UP OCCASIONALLY AND DRAW VAGUE DIAGRAMS ON THE WHITEBOARD. SOME EXAMPLES...

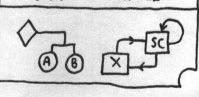

DOUG SAVAGE

How to Look Busy
lesson 4: look like crap
A BUSY WORKER IS OFTEN A STRESSED WORKER. ADOPT A LOOK OF PHYSICAL DISTRESS SO YOU LOOK OVERWORKED!
MESSY HAIR
LOOK OF PANIC
RUMPLED CLOTHES
DOUG SAVAGE

# The Afternoon Grind

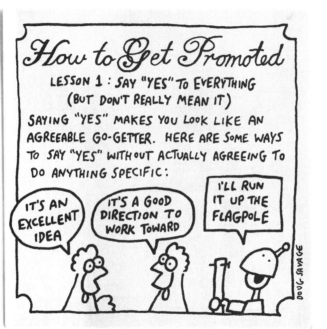

How to Get Promoted
LESSON 2: DO NOTHING
WARNING! IF YOU DO TOO MUCH ACTUAL HANDS-ON WORK, PEOPLE WILL START TO THINK OF YOU AS THAT PERSON WHO DOES ACTUAL HANDS-ON WORK.
ACTUAL WORK? HAHA NO. I'M TOO BUSY RUNNING THE STRATEGIC INITIATIVE TASK FORCE
DOUG SAVAGE

*How to Get Promoted*

LESSON 5: THE WAITING GAME

IF YOUR WORKPLACE IS PARTICULARLY AWFUL, STICK AROUND! ONE BY ONE, YOUR CO-WORKERS WILL LEAVE FOR GREENER PASTURES. EVENTUALLY, YOU'LL BE THE ONLY ONE LEFT TO PROMOTE!

DOUG-SAVAGE

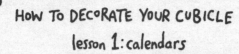

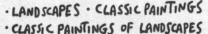

# Quitting Time

JOB SATISFACTION QUIZ!
Q: WHAT DO YOU LIKE MOST ABOUT YOUR JOB?
?
YOUR ANSWER:
IF YOU ANSWERED ONE OF THE FOLLOWING:
· THE MONEY
· IT'S EASY
· THE BENEFITS
· THE COFFEE
THEN YOU CAN DO BETTER!
DOUG SAVAGE

# Fun and Games

To grunt and sweat under a weary life, P.L.O.
But that the dread of something after death,
The undiscover'd country from whose bourn
No traveller returns, puzzles the will
And makes us rather bear those ill he
Than fly to others that we know n of
WORK ACTIVITY #19: WHITEBOARD SHAKESPEARE
WRITE SHAKESPEAREAN QUOTATIONS ON WHITEBOARDS AND LABEL THEM P.L.O. (PLEASE LEAVE ON). SEE HOW LONG THEY LAST!
DOUG SAVAGE

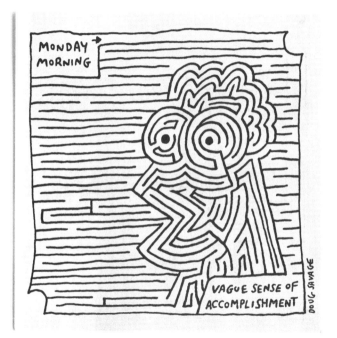

# OFFICE SCAVENGER HUNT!

## BE THE FIRST TEAM TO FIND...

A STOLEN STAPLER

A STRESS BALL

A DYING PLANT

EMAIL FROM SOMEONE TRYING TO GET YOU TO DO THEIR WORK

2 STAPLE REMOVERS

BOTTLE FROM SECRET LIQUOR STASH!

2 for 1!

EXPIRED LUNCH COUPON

CORRECTION FLUID

A SENSE OF PURPOSE

DOUG SAVAGE

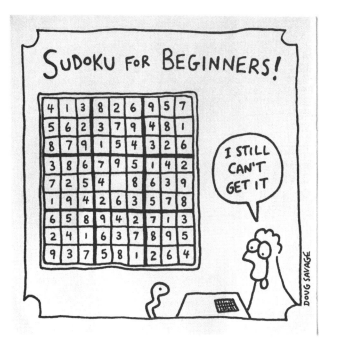

HELP THE CHICKEN MAKE IT
THROUGH THE DAY!

EXISTENTIAL CONNECT-THE-DOTS

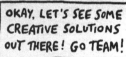

TEAM BUILDING SURVIVAL ROLEPLAY EXERCISE #2

IMAGINE THE FOLLOWING SCENARIO: WHILE SAILING IN THE MIDDLE OF THE ATLANTIC OCEAN...

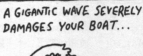

A GIGANTIC WAVE SEVERELY DAMAGES YOUR BOAT...

YOU MANAGE TO SALVAGE A RAFT AND SIX OTHER ITEMS.

AS A TEAM, RANK THE SIX ITEMS IN ORDER OF IMPORTANCE FOR YOUR SURVIVAL.

ALMA ROSA CHARDONNAY 2005

CHATEAU STE. MICHELLE 2006 REISLING

QUILCEDA CREEK 2003 CABERNET SAUVIGNON

SCHILD ESTATE 2004 SHIRAZ

BERINGER CHARDONNAY 1998

PIRATHON SHIRAZ 2005

DOUG SAVAGE

# Projects and Activities

# CREATE
## YOUR OWN
# CARTOON

~

CHANNEL YOUR
ROAD RAGE INTO
CREATIVITY BY
FILLING OUT THIS
CARTOON ON YOUR
WAY TO WORK!

# BONUS FUN!

CUT OUT AND PASTE
OVER YOUR WATCH
SO YOU CAN FEEL
LIKE THE DAY'S
ALMOST OVER
ALL DAY!

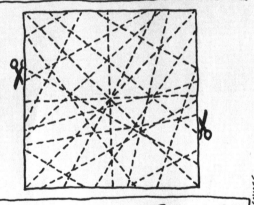

# MEETING EXEMPTION FORM

PLEASE EXCUSE _____
                              <YOUR NAME>
FROM TODAY'S MEETING BECAUSE HE/SHE
WOULD RATHER SPEND TIME ACTUALLY
DOING WORK INSTEAD OF JUST
TALKING ABOUT IT INCESSANTLY.

WARMEST REGARDS,

_____
<FAKE BOSS'S SIGNATURE>

# Stapler Labels

THIS STAPLER BELONGS TO _____

IF YOU STEAL IT, I WILL SOB UNCONTROLLABLY. FEEL GUILTY? YOU SHOULD, YOU HEARTLESS MONSTER.

**KEEP YOUR STAPLER SAFE!**

CUT OUT AND TAPE TO THE TOP OF YOUR STAPLER. IT'LL NEVER GO MISSING AGAIN!

THIS STAPLER BELONGS TO _____

YOU COULD STEAL IT, BUT FIRST YOU SHOULD KNOW THAT I TOTALLY WIPED BOOGERS ON IT.

DOUG SAVAGE

**MOCK YOUR BOSS** PASSIVE-AGGRESSIVELY USING THE POWER OF **CARTOONS**

IN THE SPEECH BUBBLE, WRITE A COMMON PHRASE THAT YOUR BOSS ALWAYS USES, THEN CUT OUT THE CARTOON AND DISPLAY IT PROMINENTLY!

YEAH, WHATEVER

DOUG SAVAGE

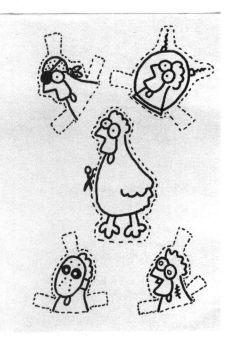

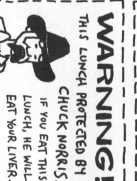

**WARNING!**

**WARNING!**

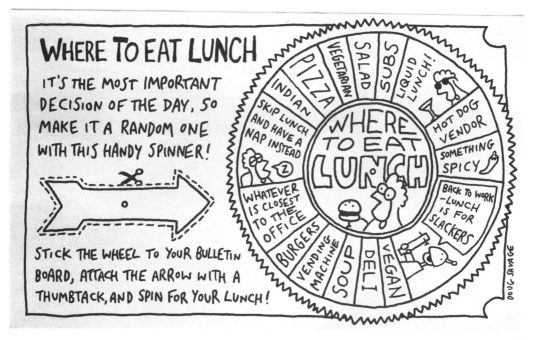

# WHERE TO EAT LUNCH

IT'S THE MOST IMPORTANT DECISION OF THE DAY, SO MAKE IT A RANDOM ONE WITH THIS HANDY SPINNER!

STICK THE WHEEL TO YOUR BULLETIN BOARD, ATTACH THE ARROW WITH A THUMBTACK, AND SPIN FOR YOUR LUNCH!

WHERE TO EAT LUNCH

PIZZA
INDIAN
SKIP LUNCH AND HAVE A NAP INSTEAD
WHATEVER IS CLOSEST TO THE OFFICE
BURGERS
VENDING MACHINE
SOUP
DELI
VEGAN
BACK TO WORK – LUNCH IS FOR SLACKERS
SOMETHING SPICY
HOT DOG VENDOR
LIQUID LUNCH!
SUBS
SALAD
VEGETARIAN

DOUG SAVAGE

# CREATE
## YOUR OWN
# CARTOON

WRITE SOMETHING
HILARIOUS IN THE
SPEECH BUBBLE, THEN
CUT OUT THE CARTOON.
CAN'T DO HILARIOUS?
GO FOR ABSURD.

**BONUS!** CUT OUT
THIS PICTURE OF
MR. T AND PASTE
IT OVER YOUR I.D.
BADGE PHOTO!

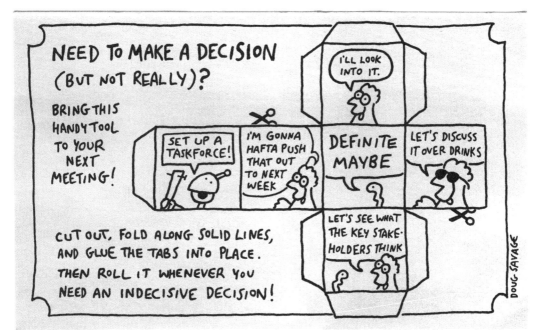

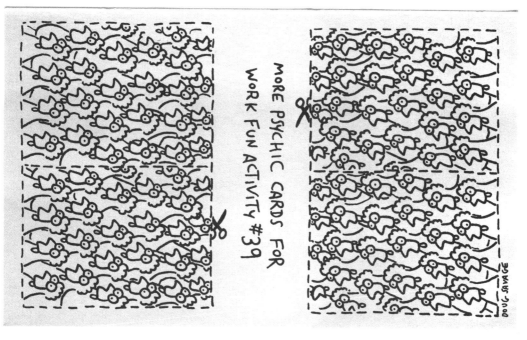

MORE PSYCHIC CARDS FOR WORK FUN ACTIVITY #39

DOUG SAVAGE

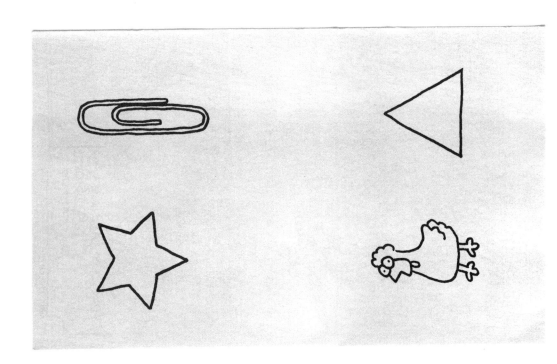

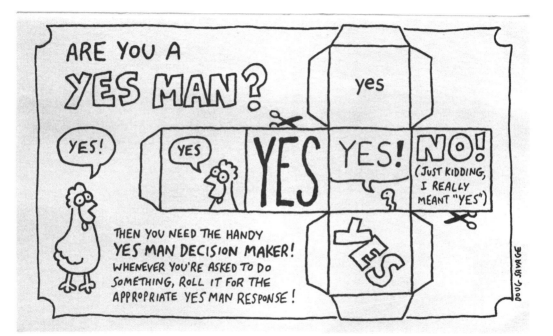

# CREATE YOUR OWN CARTOON

SOMETIMES YOU NEED PROFESSIONAL HELP. THIS IS NOT ONE OF THOSE TIMES. FILL IN THE SPEECH BUBBLE WITH YOUR OWN PSYCHIATRIC ADVICE!

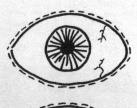

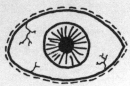

BONUS FUN!
CUT OUT AND TAPE TO
YOUR EYELIDS SO YOU
CAN HAVE A QUICK NAP.

# CREATE YOUR OWN CARTOON

FILL IN THE SPEECH BUBBLE, CUT OUT THE CARTOON, AND PROUDLY DISPLAY YOUR WORK!

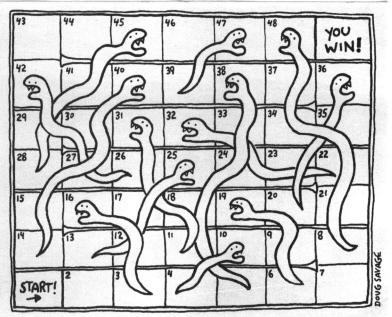

# BONUS!
## "SNAKES AND SNAKES" GAME PIECES

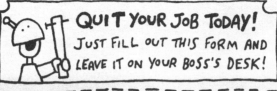

**QUIT YOUR JOB TODAY!**
JUST FILL OUT THIS FORM AND
LEAVE IT ON YOUR BOSS'S DESK!

DEAR _____,
        <BOSS'S NAME>
I REGRET TO INFORM YOU THAT I AM
RESIGNING FROM MY POSITION HERE AT
_____. THIS COMPANY IS A
<COMPANY NAME>
MISERABLE _____ AND
        <LOCATION KNOWN FOR ITS STENCH>
IF I STAY HERE MUCH LONGER, MY
_____ WILL BURST.
<VITAL ORGAN>
        SINCERELY,

_____
        <YOUR NAME>

DOUG SAVAGE

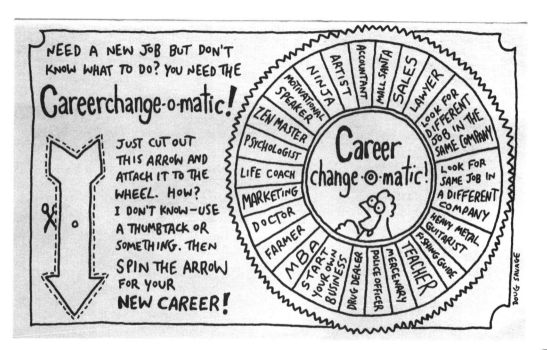

# THE GAME OF WORK
## ~ instructions ~

- CUT OUT THE FATE CARDS AND PUT THEM IN A STACK IN THE CENTER OF THE GAMEBOARD.
- CUT OUT AND ASSEMBLE THE GAME PIECES.
- START IN THE "START YOUR DAY" SPACE AND GO AROUND AND AROUND UNTIL SOMEBODY WINS.
- TO MOVE, FLIP A COIN AND MOVE ONE SPACE FOR HEADS AND TWO SPACES FOR TAILS.

DOUG SAVAGE

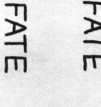

FATE

FATE

FATE

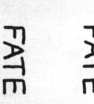

FATE

FATE

FATE

# ABOUT THE AUTHOR

By day, Doug Savage edits technical manuals for a giant corporation. But by night, he draws chicken cartoons on sticky notes. He has been drawing these Savage Chickens and posting them online every weekday since January 2005. Doug's cartoons are now read by more than half a million people every month, and appear in many books and magazines around the world. When he's not drawing chickens, Doug works on animation projects, folds origami cranes, and maintains a dazzling collection of plaid shirts. Visit his website at www.savagechickens.com.